AUTISM
SPECTRUM
DISORDERS

MENTAL ILLNESSES AND DISORDERS
Awareness and Understanding

AUTISM SPECTRUM DISORDERS

H.W. Poole

SERIES CONSULTANT

ANNE S. WALTERS, PhD

Chief Psychologist, Emma Pendleton Bradley Hospital

Clinical Associate Professor, Alpert Medical School/Brown University

MASON CREST

Mason Crest
450 Parkway Drive, Suite D
Broomall, PA 19008
www.masoncrest.com

MTM Publishing, Inc.
435 West 23rd Street, #8C
New York, NY 10011
www.mtmpublishing.com

President: Valerie Tomaselli
Vice President, Book Development: Hilary Poole
Designer: Annemarie Redmond
Copyeditor: Peter Jaskowiak
Editorial Assistant: Andrea St. Aubin

Series ISBN: 978-1-4222-3364-1
ISBN: 978-1-4222-3367-2
Ebook ISBN: 978-1-4222-8568-8

Library of Congress Cataloging-in-Publication Data

Poole, Hilary W., author.
  Autism spectrum disorders / by H.W. Poole.
      pages cm. — (Mental illnesses and disorders: awareness and understanding)
  Includes bibliographical references and index.
  ISBN 978-1-4222-3367-2 (hardback) — ISBN 978-1-4222-3364-1 (series) —
ISBN 978-1-4222-8568-8 (ebook)
  1. Autism spectrum disorders—Juvenile literature. 2. Autism—Juvenile literature. I. Title.
  RC553.A88.P66 2016
  616.85'882—dc23
                              2015006839

Printed and bound in the United States of America.

First printing
9 8 7 6 5 4 3 2 1

TABLE OF CONTENTS

Key Icons to Look for:

 Words to Understand: These words with their easy-to-understand definitions will increase the reader's understanding of the text, while building vocabulary skills.

 Sidebars: This boxed material within the main text allows readers to build knowledge, gain insights, explore possibilities, and broaden their perspectives by weaving together additional information to provide realistic and holistic perspectives.

 Research Projects: Readers are pointed toward areas of further inquiry connected to each chapter. Suggestions are provided for projects that encourage deeper research and analysis.

 Text-Dependent Questions: These questions send the reader back to the text for more careful attention to the evidence presented there.

 Series Glossary of Key Terms: This back-of-the-book glossary contains terminology used throughout the series. Words found here increase the reader's ability to read and comprehend higher-level books and articles in this field.

People who cope with mental illnesses and disorders deserve our empathy and respect.

(istockphoto/digitalskillet)

Introduction to the Series

According to the National Institute of Mental Health, in 2012 there were an estimated 45 million people in the United States suffering from mental illness, or 19 percent of all US adults. A separate 2011 study found that among children, almost one in five suffer from some form of mental illness or disorder. The nature and level of impairment varies widely. For example, children and adults with anxiety disorders may struggle with a range of symptoms, from a constant state of worry about both real and imagined events to a complete inability to leave the house. Children or adults with schizophrenia might experience periods when the illness is well controlled by medication and therapies, but there may also be times when they must spend time in a hospital for their own safety and the safety of others. For every person with mental illness who makes the news, there are many more who do not, and these are the people that we must learn more about and help to feel accepted, and even welcomed, in this world of diversity.

It is not easy to have a mental illness in this country. Access to mental health services remains a significant issue. Many states and some private insurers have "opted out" of providing sufficient coverage for mental health treatment. This translates to limits on the amount of sessions or frequency of treatment, inadequate rates for providers, and other problems that make it difficult for people to get the care they need.

Meanwhile, stigma about mental illness remains widespread. There are still whispers about "bad parenting," or "the other side of the tracks." The whisperers imply that mental illness is something you bring upon yourself, or something that someone does to you. Obviously, mental illness can be exacerbated by an adverse event such as trauma or parental instability. But there is just as much truth to the biological bases of mental illness. No one is made schizophrenic by ineffective parenting, for example, or by engaging in "wild" behavior as an adolescent. Mental illness is a complex interplay of genes, biology, and the environment, much like many physical illnesses.

People with mental illness are brave soldiers, really. They fight their illness every day, in all of the settings of their lives. When people with an anxiety disorder graduate from college, you know that they worked very hard to get there—harder, perhaps, than those who did not struggle with a psychiatric issue. They got up every day with a pit in their stomach about facing the world, and they worried about their finals more than their classmates. When they had to give a presentation in class, they thought their world was going to end and that they would faint, or worse, in front of everyone. But they fought back, and they kept going. Every day. That's bravery, and that is to be respected and congratulated.

These books were written to help young people get the facts about mental illness. Facts go a long way to dispel stigma. Knowing the facts gives students the opportunity to help others to know and understand. If your student lives with someone with mental illness, these books can help students know a bit more about what to expect. If they are concerned about someone, or even about themselves, these books are meant to provide some answers and a place to start.

The topics covered in this series are those that seem most relevant for middle schoolers—disorders that they are most likely to come into contact with or to be curious about. Schizophrenia is a rare illness, but it is an illness with many misconceptions and inaccurate portrayals in media. Anxiety and depressive disorders, on the other hand, are quite common. Most of our youth have likely had personal experience of anxiety or depression, or knowledge of someone who struggles with these symptoms.

As a teacher or a librarian, thank you for taking part in dispelling myths and bringing facts to your children and students. Thank you for caring about the brave soldiers who live and work with mental illness. These reference books are for all of them, and also for those of us who have the good fortune to work with and know them.

—Anne S. Walters, PhD
Chief Psychologist, Emma Pendleton Bradley Hospital
Clinical Professor, Alpert Medical School/Brown University

CHAPTER ONE

UNDERSTANDING AUTISM SPECTRUM DISORDERS

Words to Understand

empathy: understanding the feelings of others.

obsess: to focus completely on a particular thing.

pervasive: widespread.

socialization: the way a person behaves with others.

spectrum: range.

Tracy's birth was a dream come true for her parents. She was a happy baby, and everything seemed normal at first. But soon after Tracy turned one, her mom started to notice that Tracy was different from other kids her age. Other babies were cuddly, giving kisses and hugs to their moms. They were constantly exploring—crawling, touching things, and putting things in their mouths. They even tried to talk. Even if it was mostly babble, they were trying to communicate.

Tracy wasn't like that. She didn't want to be held. She didn't make eye contact. Tracy would stay on one part of the carpet, disinterested in other people. Sometimes, she'd rock back and forth for long periods of time.

"It's like I'm invisible," her mom told Tracy's doctor. "She looks right through me."

The arrival of a baby is an exciting and emotional time for the whole family.

SYMPTOMS

The signs of autism include:

- a significant delay in learning to talk
- an unwillingness or inability to make eye contact
- a dislike of being touched or hugged
- difficulty with "regular," back-and-forth conversations
- difficulty understanding the facial expressions of others
- difficulty using facial expressions or gestures to communicate
- difficulty expressing **empathy**
- inflexibility, such as becoming very upset when a routine changes
- repetitive movements, such as rocking back and forth
- repeating words or sounds
- extreme reactions to how things taste, sound, or look

Keep in mind that having just one or two of these symptoms does not mean a person has autism. Also, not every person with autism has every symptom—the disorder can look different from person to person.

The doctor examined Tracy and gave her parents the difficult news. More tests were needed, but it was very likely that Tracy had autism.

Defining Autism

Autism is a disorder that affects two important parts of human development: communication and **socialization**. In other words,

According to the group Autism Speaks, the disorder costs a family an average of $60,000 per year.

it affects how we interact with others. Autism can also affect how a person learns and how his or her imagination works.

The word *autism* comes from the Ancient Greek word *autos,* which means "self." (For example, an *autobiography* is a biography written by the person who lived it.) The disorder was defined by Dr. Leo Kanner. In 1943, Kanner wrote a paper in which he described the symptoms we now call autism. Before that time, kids with autism were often considered to be just "slow," "strange," or even "crazy."

The Spectrum

Autism can have a wide range of impacts on different people. Some need a lot of help, even with simple daily activities.

Occasionally, the disorder is so severe that the person can't speak at all. On the other hand, many people with autism grow up to have "regular" lives—they have jobs and hobbies, families and friends, all the things you'd expect. In fact, you might not even know someone has autism unless she tells you. Because of this variation, autism's official name is autism spectrum disorder (ASD). The word **spectrum** lets us know that people with autism can vary greatly from one another.

In a rainbow, the colors yellow and violet are two points on the color spectrum. But yellow is not better than violet—it's just different. The same is true with ASD. You might have heard an adult say that a particular person is "on the spectrum." That expression just means the person has autism in some form. No point on the spectrum is "better" than any other. They are just different.

Asperger's Syndrome

In 1944 an Austrian doctor named Hans Asperger noticed that a few children in his practice had very similar symptoms: they had normal or even high intelligence, but they were socially isolated. They were unable to relate to other kids and had a hard time making "regular" conversation. These patients were both physically and socially clumsy. Dr. Asperger wrote about these patients, describing their problems as a "personality disorder." It was many years before his work was noticed. Although Dr. Asperger did not name the syndrome after himself, when his writings

DID YOU KNOW?

Estimates vary, but autism may affect as many as 1 in 68 children in the United States.

were translated into English, his name became forever associated with the disorder.

Asperger's syndrome used to be viewed as separate from autism. Over time, however, doctors realized that the two disorders are actually related. Today, Asperger's syndrome is not considered to be a separate diagnosis from ASD. But some people call it "high-functioning autism." This term refers to

Temple Grandin is a scientist, author, and autism activist. One of her inventions is the "hug machine," which was designed to comfort people with ASD.

AUTISM AND THE *DSM-5*

When treating people with mental disorders, doctors refer to a guide called the *Diagnostic and Statistical Manual of Mental Disorders* (*DSM*). This manual is revised frequently, to make sure that it reflects current ideas about mental illness. The manual has been revised five times so far. The most recent edition was published in 2013.

In earlier editions of the *DSM*, a number of disorders—Asperger's syndrome, childhood disintegrative disorder, autistic disorder, and pervasive developmental disorder not otherwise specified (PDD-NOS)—were considered to be separate but related disorders. Each of these was part of a larger category called "**pervasive** developmental disorders." But the *DSM-5* treats all these conditions as simply points on the broader autism spectrum. The older terms are still common in daily life, however. You may hear about someone who has Asperger's or PDD-NOS. But the *DSM-5* does not view them separately.

the fact that people with Asperger's can achieve a great deal despite their disorder.

People that used to be identified with Asperger's tend to be very bright, but they can also be very limited in their interests. They often **obsess** over one particular thing. Sometimes people with Asperger's are described as "little professors," because they are so eager to share what they know. Someone with Asperger's might know absolutely everything there is to know about trains, for example. But he may not notice or care whether you are interested in hearing about it.

People with Asperger's sometimes have trouble getting along with others. But they also have huge gifts to offer, due to their high intelligence and intense focus. As the scientist and autism advocate Temple Grandin said in 2013,

If we got rid of . . . autism, well, you wouldn't even have any computers. You wouldn't have any electricity. Who do you think made the first stone spear? It wasn't the social yakety-yaks around the campfire, that's for sure.

Many of our great geniuses—especially in scientific and technical fields—may have had Asperger's.

Text-Dependent Questions

1. What key parts of human development are affected by autism?
2. Why do we talk about a "spectrum" of autism?
3. What are the characteristics of someone with Asperger's syndrome?

Research Project

A lot has been written about geniuses of history and whether or not they had autism spectrum disorder. Not everyone agrees, but some historians have argued that Archimedes, Charles Lindbergh, Albert Einstein, and Gregor Mendel may have been "on the spectrum." Read a biography of one of these people. Do you agree with the opinion that the person may have had ASD? Why or why not?

CHAPTER TWO

MAJOR SYMPTOMS OF ASD

 Words to Understand

cues: signals.

hypersensitive: too sensitive.

involuntary: automatic.

literal: describing someone who understands the world in a concrete way, without much imagination.

subjective: not based on observation; affected by personal feelings.

It's important to remember that ASD expresses itself differently in different people. And you can't know what is going on in people's minds just by looking at them.

If you have a broken arm, it will be obvious to any doctor. If you have chicken pox, you'll know it. Autism is not like that. True, in certain people the symptoms are so severe that there is no doubt. But for most people, things aren't so obvious.

After all, a lot of the symptoms are **subjective**. For example, one symptom is "inflexibility." But what seems like inflexibility to one person might seem like harmless stubbornness to someone else. Sometimes it can be difficult to tell the difference between a symptom and a personality trait. Usually, we call something a "symptom" when it creates big challenges in the person's life. Autism symptoms can make life very difficult—both for the person with the disorder and for that person's families, friends, and teachers.

Another thing to understand about ASD symptoms is that they vary a lot among different people. That's why we talk about a "spectrum" when it comes to autism. No two people with ASD are completely alike. However, a few classic symptoms are shared by a great many people with ASD.

Right Words at the Right Time

Although every person is unique, we do know that all humans follow the same general pattern of growth. For example, most babies can recognize their own names by the time they are seven months old. Some babies might do that a little earlier, and some a little later. But seven months is more or less the expected moment. We also know that most one-year-olds can say at least a word or two, while most three-year-olds can speak sentences of a few words.

The earliest signs of ASD usually involve delays in speech and social skills.

One of the most important warning signs of ASD is "language delay." That's the term for when a child does not meet the general timeline of development. Delayed speech does not definitely mean that a child has ASD. However, it is a sign that there *might* be a problem. The good news is, studies have shown that many kids with language delay can catch up if the problem is addressed early.

It's All Over Your Face

If you play a card game, watch your opponent's face closely. When she draws a card from the deck, the expression on her face might reveal whether she got a good card or not. Card players call this "a tell"—an **involuntary** expression or gesture that *tells* you what the person is thinking.

This idea of the "tell" isn't just for cards. We rely on "tells" all the time. Sometimes they are called social **cues** or nonverbal communication. Facial expressions, gestures, and tones of voice are all ways we tell each other things without using words.

Let's say you have a really strange dream. At school the next day, you try to explain to a friend how weird the dream was. But your friend's eyes start to wander. Maybe he sighs or starts looking through his backpack. These are all "tells" that your friend is not so interested in your dream. Seeing these cues might cause you to cut the story short.

On the other hand, maybe your friend smiles and nods. He puts down his backpack and looks right at you. These are cues that he wants to hear more about your dream.

Most of us don't even think about nonverbal communication. We respond to it without even noticing. But what seems obvious to you is not always obvious to people with ASD. They often don't recognize the cues that are a natural part of daily conversation. They have to consciously learn how to recognize facial expressions. But when they do, people with ASD can practice responding to social cues in useful ways.

I Feel You

Did you ever ask a friend, "Are you okay?" Maybe the friend shrugged sadly and said, "I'm fine." Which did you believe

Nonverbal cues can signal our interest or disinterest in a conversation.

more: the word "fine" or the sad shrug? Chances are, you knew that the shrug was more honest than the word.

Nonverbal communication is very useful for expressing feelings. In fact, it's often better than words. But for people with autism, these emotional cues are not any clearer than the social cues mentioned above.

People with autism have trouble recognizing the emotional expressions of others. But it's important to understand that they aren't "unfeeling." It's more that their brains don't catch all the emotional signals that most of us catch. For people with autism, it can seem like everyone else "talks" in an unspoken and mysterious code.

Sometimes you can tell someone how you feel without speaking.

When a Box Is Just a Box

Have you ever seen kittens play with yarn? Or puppies chase a ball? These young animals are playing, but their play has a purpose. They are practicing skills—such as hunting and chasing—that they will need later. Of course, nowadays we keep our cats and dogs pretty well fed. But when animals are in the wild, these skills are the difference between life and death. And the skills are all usually learned through play.

Kids play, too, and like puppies and kittens, kids practice important skills with their games. Play helps kids practice how to wait their turn, how to compromise, and how to handle disappointment when they lose. Play is a very important part of human development.

Kids with ASD may be more likely to arrange their toys than play with them in a more imaginative way.

Here's the problem: some kids with ASD don't understand how to play. Their minds tend to be much more **literal** than most. A kid who sees an empty box might imagine that it's a rocket ship. Or maybe it's a castle, robot, or getaway car. A kid with ASD is more likely to think, "Hmm, a box." Instead of playing pretend with stuffed animals, a kid with ASD is more likely to line up the animals in alphabetical order.

This creates several problems. First, of course, it's harder for kids with ASD to understand what other kids are doing or talking about. And second, kids with ASD don't get to practice all those skills that others learn through play. Therapy for kids with ASD often involves helping their imaginations stretch and grow. With help and practice, kids with ASD can be ready to ride that rocket ship, too.

System Overload

As we said, people with autism tend to miss a lot of social cues. But that doesn't mean that they don't notice a whole lot of other things. In fact, another classic symptom of autism is **hypersensitivity**.

Have you ever had been bothered by the tag in the back of a shirt? It's annoying. You might fidget, trying to adjust where the tag touches you. Maybe you ask an adult to cut the tag out. But for people with autism, sensations like that tag are not just annoying. People with autism can be so sensitive that they might get very upset. They might find it impossible to concentrate on *anything* except the uncomfortable shirt.

Different people can be sensitive to different things. Some people with autism are disturbed by particular sounds, tastes, textures, or smells.

Old Habits

We all have certain things that we want to be a certain way. We know the "best" route to school. We have a favorite chair we always sit in to watch TV. Or a favorite pair of socks we always wear on specific days. Habits and rituals make us feel safe in an uncertain world.

But sometimes there's construction on the road to school. Or someone else is sitting in our chair. Sometimes our favorite socks are in the washing machine. But that's okay. We might not like it, but we adjust.

Some people with ASD are extremely sensitive to particular tastes, textures, or smells. This can make dinner a challenging experience at times.

"WON'T" VERSUS "CAN'T"

It's important to remember that a symptom is not a choice. Someone who has a stubborn personality can, with effort, get their reactions under control. People with autism aren't being "stubborn." Their disorder simply makes it difficult for them to adjust to change.

People with autism often can't adjust, or can only adjust with great difficulty. What most of us would see as a minor annoyance ("Argh, my favorite socks are in the wash") can be incredibly upsetting to them. For example, a child with autism might insist that the family drive the same way to school every day, no matter what. Or he might be terribly upset if there is a substitute teacher he wasn't expecting. Repetition and familiarity are extremely important to many people with ASD.

Text-Dependent Questions

1. What are some classic symptoms of ASD?
2. What is hypersensitivity?
3. What are some examples of nonverbal communication?

Research Project

Take a few minutes to sit quietly in a public place, like a restaurant, park, or your school library. Look at the people around you and see if you can guess what they might be thinking or feeling. What can you learn about people just from watching them? How do their faces, expressions, and gestures express their thoughts and feelings?

CHAPTER THREE

CAUSES OF ASD

 Words to Understand

cluster: grouped closely together.

genetic: relating to heredity.

immune: not affected by something.

innate: existing from the beginning.

mutation: in genetics, a change in the structure of a gene.

retract: to take back.

toxin: a poison.

trigger: something that causes something else to happen.

Chapter one mentioned Dr. Leo Kanner, who was the first to describe the condition we now call autism spectrum disorder (ASD). In addition to describing the symptoms, Dr. Kanner made another important contribution to our understanding of autism.

In his 1943 paper, Dr. Kanner described the condition as "**innate**." That is, he suspected that people with autism were *born with* the condition. He noticed that autistic traits seemed to be more common in some families than in others. This observation led him to consider possible **genetic** causes.

These days, describing a mental condition as innate is not very controversial. But when Dr. Kanner was writing, most people believed that mental problems were caused by experiences in childhood. In fact, doctors used to believe

Doctors no longer believe that parents are the cause of ASD.

that autism was caused by parents who didn't love their children. This idea even had a nickname: "refrigerator mothers," or those who were cold to their children, were blamed for causing the disorder.

Genetics and Autism

We now know that Dr. Kanner's idea that autism is innate was correct. One or several genetic **mutations** play at least some role in ASD.

Studies have found that if one identical twin has ASD, the other twin will also have the disorder at least 70 percent of the time. This is strong evidence for a genetic link. But it also means that 30 percent of the time, one twin has ASD while the other does not. So whatever the genetic link might be, it is not a simple one.

Here's something fascinating: even if both twins have ASD, they can have different symptoms. For example, one may have more challenges with language skills, while the other might have more challenges with emotional skills. We said earlier that ASD can look different from one person to another. In fact, the disorder can look different from one twin to another!

There are several reasons why this might be true. First, brain development is extremely complex. We are only beginning to understand how and why brains develop the way they do. It's possible that identical twins could have the same genetic mutation, but the mutation could express itself in different ways.

It's also likely that ASD has a secondary cause. That is, maybe it's not genetics alone, but rather genetics plus some other factor. A person's genetics might make him or her more *at risk* for ASD, but it might be something else that **triggers** the

DID YOU KNOW?

The "refrigerator mother" theory has been denied *almost* everywhere . . . but not France! Many French doctors believe that parents are at least partly to blame if their children have ASD.

Researchers often study twins when they are trying to understand the possible genetic causes of disorders.

disorder. For whatever reason, one twin might have been more strongly influenced by that trigger than the other.

Environment and Autism

When you think about the word *environment*, you might think about air or water pollution. And in fact, **toxins** from the environment may be a trigger for ASD. Autism cases are known to **cluster** around particular geographical areas. This has led some researchers to wonder if something in the environment—such as a toxin—causes autism rates to rise in that community. But so far, no specific toxin has been proven to cause ASD.

When doctors talk about "environmental" causes of ASD, they don't just mean air, water, and so on. They also mean the whole context in which a baby develops. For example, the children of older parents (meaning age 40 and up) are a bit more likely to develop ASD. Folic acid, a substance in food that's vital to brain development, might have a role to play. Pregnant women who are low in folic acid may be more likely to have autistic children. Being born premature at a very low weight might also be associated with developing ASD later on. Research continues on all these environmental factors.

Vaccines and Autism

As you can see, there is a lot we don't know about the causes of ASD. This is very frustrating, both for doctors and for families.

RACE, ETHNICITY, AND AUTISM SPECTRUM DISORDER

ASD has been found in kids of every ethnic background. However, white children are somewhat more likely to be diagnosed with ASD than kids of other races. We don't yet know whether white children are truly more at risk for ASD. In many parts of the United States, whites tend to have better access to health care. This lack of access might affect our understanding of how many kids of other races have ASD. That is, it's possible other kids do get ASD at the same rates as whites, but they aren't diagnosed at the same rates.

People want answers. Parents of very young children want to know if there is anything they can do to protect their babies.

Unfortunately, widespread fear can cause people to jump to conclusions. We want answers so badly that we are tempted to believe anything that "seems right." This has definitely been the case when it comes to the issue of autism and vaccines.

In 1998, a study was published in a British medical journal called *The Lancet*. The study seemed to suggest a connection between a common childhood vaccine and symptoms of ASD. Although the study was very small—it only involved 12 children—it led to a panic.

The symptoms of ASD tend to appear when kids are around three years old. This also is when kids get a lot of vaccinations. So the idea that the two events were connected "seemed right"

THE FIRST VACCINE

Smallpox is a deadly virus that has killed hundreds of millions of people. In fact, some historians have argued that smallpox killed more people than every other virus *combined*.

In the 1790s, an English doctor named Edward Jenner figured out that by exposing someone to a tiny amount of a less harmful version of the virus, that person would become **immune** to the deadlier version. At first, people mocked Jenner's idea. But, in time, the wisdom of vaccinating people became clear—Jenner's idea has saved an uncountable number of human lives. And thanks to vaccination, smallpox was wiped out in the late 1970s.

The Centers for Disease Control and Prevention recommends vaccinating against a large number of diseases, including diphtheria, tetanus, pertussis (whooping cough), measles, mumps, rubella, hepatitis A and B, and varicella (chicken pox).

to a lot of parents. Before long, books and web sites were echoing the claims of the study. Self-proclaimed experts went on television to warn parents about the "danger" of vaccines. Congress even held hearings on the topic.

But meanwhile, no other studies were able to re-create the results of that 1998 *Lancet* study. In time, it became clear why: the *Lancet* study was a fraud. It claimed that the children had developed ASD symptoms within days of vaccination, but that turned out to be untrue. The main author of the study had misrepresented his results.

The Lancet **retracted** the study in 2011, saying that it's "utterly clear, without any ambiguity at all, that the statements in the paper were utterly false." A doctor named D. K. Flaherty called the *Lancet* study "the most damaging medical hoax of the last 100 years."

It's very painful for parents to see their children struggle with ASD. It can feel even worse when the cause is unknown.

WHAT SEEMS TRUE

Undertakers use a substance called formaldehyde to help keep dead people looking presentable for their funerals. Scientists preserve specimens in a formaldehyde solution called formalin. So when people hear that formaldehyde is also used in certain vaccines, they tend to panic. Sticking your baby sister with a needle of the same stuff that's used for dead things? It seems like a bad idea, doesn't it?

Here's what you probably didn't know: you have formaldehyde in your body right now. Everyone does! In fact, the human body uses formaldehyde in normal bodily processes. So while the word might *sound* scary, there is actually more to the story. The lesson is: what "seems" true isn't always the whole truth.

But there is no scientific evidence that vaccines are involved. The group Autism Speaks says that it "strongly encourage(s) parents to have their children vaccinated for protection against serious disease."

Text-Dependent Questions

1. What do identical twins tell us about ASD?
2. How might genes be involved in the development of ASD?
3. What are some environmental factors that might play a role?

Research Project

Find out more about Edward Jenner and his smallpox vaccine. Why did people react so badly to the idea at first? How has Jenner's work been improved upon by modern scientists? What other diseases have been brought under control with vaccination?

CHAPTER FOUR

LIVING WITH ASD

Words to Understand

comorbidity: two or more illnesses appearing at the same time.

conclusive: certain, definitive.

gastrointestinal: relating to the stomach and digestion.

maladaptive: describing an unhelpful response to a particular situation or problem.

misdiagnosis: an incorrect identification of a patient's problem.

If you ever hear someone promise that he has a "cure" for ASD, get ready—he is about to "sell" you something. There is no cure for autism.

However, there are lots of things people can do to *manage* their autism. People who have severe ASD may always need extra help. But the majority of people with ASD can learn to handle the challenges of their disorder and have great, independent lives.

Early Detection

It is very important for people with ASD to get help as soon as possible. Children who are diagnosed earlier in life can get access to treatment earlier, and this leads to better outcomes.

When parents suspect that their child may have a problem, it is important to find a team of professionals that is experienced with diagnosing autism. Some doctors think that observing a child in their office for an hour is enough to make a diagnosis. But ASD experts prefer more specific tools, such as the Autism Diagnostic Observation Schedule and the Autism Diagnostic Interview. Doctors need special training to be able to use these tools. These extra methods of evaluation help doctors understand the specifics of a particular kid's problems. They also help prevent **misdiagnosis**.

Once children are diagnosed, they are then sent for treatment. Because every person with ASD is different, every person's therapy must be different, as well. Experts tailor programs to the specific needs of the individual.

Early Intervention. All states have programs for children who show delays in development from infancy until age three. These programs usually evaluate all aspects of a child's development.

Opposite page: Mental health professionals can use the Autism Diagnostic Observation Schedule to try and figure out if their patients have ASD.

They then help develop plans for the children and the families to help their developmental progress. Referrals for these programs usually come from pediatricians. Since they are usually the first professionals to interact with a child, they can help parents decide whether a child is developing as expected.

Individualized Education Plans (IEPs). Just because a kid has ASD, that does not mean she can't be successful in school. Parents can work with schools to create an IEP. This plan can involve special attention in class, additional teaching outside the regular classroom, and frequent monitoring of the student's progress.

Some teachers are specially trained in ASD. Their techniques can make a huge impact in the lives of kids with the disorder. Children are usually referred to special education directly from early intervention programs. Programs for people with developmental delays start at age 3 and can go all the way to age 21.

Specially designed programs can help kids with ASD get the most out of their education.

Behavioral Therapy. It is not a cure, but behavioral therapy can be extremely helpful in improving the lives of people with ASD. The younger the person is when therapy starts, the better off he or she will be in the long run. Therapists can help kids improve their language, communication, learning, and coping skills. Some families also get therapy to learn strategies to help their family member manage his ASD.

A particular kind of behavior therapy, called applied behavior analysis, or ABA, is especially good at helping children with autism learn language and social skills. ABA programs are supervised by doctors or educators who have special training. The programs can be very intensive, taking up to 30 hours a week.

Other types of therapy include speech and language therapy, occupational therapy, counseling services, and psychiatry.

Extra Challenges

When it comes to ASD, the concept of **comorbidity** is important. That's a scary-sounding term, but it just means that people can have more than one disorder at a time. Several disorders are very common for people who also have ASD. Often, managing autism begins with managing these other troubles first.

Sleep Problems. It is also common for people with ASD to have trouble sleeping. In fact, as many as 80 percent of kids with ASD may have at least some trouble sleeping at some point. Sometimes kids with ASD have trouble with their circadian rhythm—the internal system that tells us when to wake up and when to sleep. Keeping a regular schedule of sleep times and waking times can do a lot to help people sleep.

Sometimes physical problems keep kids with ASD awake. Be sure and mention the problem at the next doctor visit.

Stomach Problems. **Gastrointestinal** problems are very common among people with ASD. A number of studies have found that kids who have ASD are more likely to have stomach problems than kids who don't.

Sometimes these problems result from the autism. For example, someone might be very sensitive to the taste, smell, or texture of particular foods. This might lead that person to have a very limited diet, which can cause digestion problems. Doctors call this **maladaptive** behavior: the ASD symptoms lead a person to make choices that are bad for her physical health. Improving the diet—for example, getting more fiber by eating more fruits, vegetables, and whole grains—can help ease these problems.

Some people believe that ASD is not caused by stomach problems, but that it can be made worse by gastrointestinal problems. A fairly recent trend involves managing ASD through diet. One popular diet is called GFCF, which stands for gluten free, casein free. Gluten is found in wheat (and many other products), and casein is found in dairy. Someone on a GFCF diet must *not* eat bread, pasta, cookies, milk, ice cream, or cheese. She also has to be careful about taking vitamins, which often contain gluten. So do many toothpastes—even if you don't eat the toothpaste, bits of it can still be absorbed into your body.

DID YOU KNOW?

About 36 percent of kids with ASD also have some sort of food allergy. Compare that to kids without ASD: only about 8 percent of them have food allergies.

PLAN FOR PROBLEMS

People with ASD have trouble adjusting to change. The more routine they have in their lives, the better off they are. This could mean anything from predictable schedules to predictable menus. All these routines help people with ASD lower their anxiety.

But as we all know, life is not always predictable. Eventually, we might be unable to follow some part of our routine. It's a good idea to talk through what happens next. Have some plans in mind for what happens if a loved one with ASD is upset by sudden change.

A number of studies have been conducted on GFCF diets and autism. So far, there is no **conclusive** proof that the diet works. Some studies have found no improvement at all, while a few others have found evidence that certain kids with ASD might benefit. Kids who have ASD and gastrointestinal problems gain the most from dietary changes.

Some parents report that their children's autism got a lot better with the GFCF diet. Some experts have wondered if a healthier diet overall—with less sugar, fat, and processed foods—might be the real source of the improvement. Of course, children without autism might have food allergies, and a dietary change can be helpful in these cases as well. But everyone can agree that we need more study of GFCF and the role of diet in general.

IMPORTANT DIET ADVICE

It is important for parents to work closely with their pediatrician and other treatment providers when making dietary changes. When you take dairy out of your diet, you are taking out a major source of calcium. Calcium is hugely important for kids, because it helps bones grow strong. Young people on a GFCF diet need to be very careful to replace all the nutrients they lose. For example, broccoli and kale are two good sources of calcium. These green vegetables also contain fiber, which is also important if whole grains are avoided.

Anxiety and Depression. Go back and look at the classic symptoms of ASD in chapter one. It's not hard to imagine why many people with ASD also have anxiety. If you couldn't understand the social cues around you, you'd be pretty anxious, too. If you were hypersensitive to noises or textures, or if you had trouble understanding the things people say, the world might seem like a very threatening place.

Depression is also a common problem for people with ASD. And, again, it's not hard to understand why. People with ASD sometimes have trouble making friends—but that doesn't mean they don't want friends! ASD can make people feel very isolated and lonely. Kids with ASD may feel very frustrated in school. Sometimes they feel that they will never be "normal" the way other kids are. This can easily lead to depression. It is also possible that some of these psychiatric symptoms are caused by some of the brain differences that we expect in people with autism.

The good news is, there is lots of help and hope for people with depression and anxiety, whether they have ASD or not. Talking to a doctor or counselor is a good start. Sometimes a low dosage of medication can make a huge difference for people with ASD. (You might also check out two other books in this set, *Anxiety Disorders* and *Depression*, for more tips on coping with these problems.)

Text-Dependent Questions

1. What kinds of help can benefit kids with ASD?
2. What is the relationship between gastrointestinal problems and ASD?
3. Why are anxiety and depression problems for people with ASD?

Research Project

Find out what services your school and community offer for people with ASD and write up a report. You might start by interviewing someone in your school's special education department. Ask what types of special needs kids with ASD have, and what your school does to help them. You might also search the Internet for "autism spectrum disorder" and the name of your town to see what is available. You can also check the resource guides at web sites like Autism Speaks (www.autismspeaks.org/family-services/resource-guide).

Further Reading

BOOKS

Grandin, Temple, and Richard Panek. *The Autistic Brain: Helping Different Kinds of Minds Succeed.* Boston: Houghton Mifflin Harcourt, 2014.

Notbohm, Ellen. *Ten Things Every Child with Autism Wishes You Knew.* Updated ed. Arlington, TX: Future Horizons, 2012.

Rodger, Margeurite. *Autism Spectrum Disorder.* Understanding Mental Health. New York: Crabtree, 2014.

Siegel, Bryna. *Helping Children with Autism Learn.* New York: Oxford University Press, 2003.

ONLINE

Autism Speaks. "What Is Autism?" http://www.autismspeaks.org/what-autism.

Centers for Disease Control and Prevention. "Kids Quest: Autism." http://www.cdc.gov/ncbddd/kids/autism.html.

Grandin, Temple. "The Autistic Brain." Video from the Chicago Humanities Festival. 2013. http://youtu.be/MWePrOuSeSY.

Smith, Melinda, Jeanne Sega, and Ted Hutman. "Helping Children with Autism." Helpguide. org. http://www.helpguide.org/articles/autism/helping-children-with-autism.htm.

LOSING HOPE?

This free, confidential phone number will connect you to counselors who can help.

National Suicide Prevention Lifeline

1-800-273-TALK (1-800-273-8255)

Series Glossary

acute: happening powerfully for a short period of time.

affect: as a noun, the way someone seems on the outside—including attitude, emotion, and voice (pronounced with the emphasis on the first syllable, "AFF-eckt").

atypical: different from what is usually expected.

bipolar: involving two, opposite ends.

chronic: happening again and again over a long period of time.

comorbidity: two or more illnesses appearing at the same time.

correlation: a relationship or connection.

delusion: a false belief with no connection to reality.

dementia: a mental disorder, featuring severe memory loss.

denial: refusal to admit that there is a problem.

depressant: a substance that slows down bodily functions.

depression: a feeling of hopelessness and lack of energy.

deprivation: a hurtful lack of something important.

diagnose: to identify a problem.

empathy: understanding someone else's situation and feelings.

epidemic: a widespread illness.

euphoria: a feeling of extreme, even overwhelming, happiness.

hallucination: something a person sees or hears that is not really there.

heredity: the passing of a trait from parents to children.

hormone: a substance in the body that helps it function properly.

hypnotic: a type of drug that causes sleep.

impulsivity: the tendency to act without thinking.

inattention: distraction; not paying attention.

insomnia: inability to fall asleep and/or stay asleep.

licensed: having an official document proving one is capable with a certain set of skills.

manic: a high level of excitement or energy.

misdiagnose: to incorrectly identify a problem.

moderation: limited in amount, not extreme.

noncompliance: refusing to follow rules or do as instructed.

onset: the beginning of something; pronounced like "on" and "set."

outpatient: medical care that happens while a patient continues to live at home.

overdiagnose: to determine more people have a certain illness than actually do.

pediatricians: doctors who treat children and young adults.

perception: awareness or understanding of reality.

practitioner: a person who actively participates in a particular field.

predisposition: to be more likely to do something, either due to your personality or biology.

psychiatric: having to do with mental illness.

psychiatrist: a medical doctor who specializes in mental disorders.

psychoactive: something that has an effect on the mind and behavior.

psychosis: a severe mental disorder where the person loses touch with reality.

psychosocial: the interaction between someone's thoughts and the outside world of relationships.

psychotherapy: treatment for mental disorders.

relapse: getting worse after a period of getting better.

spectrum: a range; in medicine, from less extreme to more extreme.

stereotype: a simplified idea about a type of person, not connected to actual individuals.

stimulant: a substance that speeds up bodily functions.

therapy: treatment of a problem; can be done with medicine or simply by talking with a therapist.

trigger: something that causes something else.

Index

Page numbers in *italics* refer to photographs.

About the Author

H. W. POOLE is a writer and editor of books for young people, such as the *Horrors of History* series (Charlesbridge). She is also responsible for many critically acclaimed reference books, including *Political Handbook of the World* (CQ Press) and the *Encyclopedia of Terrorism* (SAGE). She was coauthor and editor of the *History of the Internet* (ABC-CLIO), which won the 2000 American Library Association RUSA award.

About the Advisor

ANNE S. WALTERS is Clinical Associate Professor of Psychiatry and Human Behavior. She is the Clinical Director of the Children's Partial Hospital Program at Bradley Hospital, a program that provides partial hospital level of care for children ages 7–12 and their families. She also serves as Chief Psychologist for Bradley Hospital. She is actively involved in teaching activities within the Clinical Psychology Training Programs of the Alpert Medical School of Brown University and serves as Child Track Seminar Co-Coordinator. Dr. Walters completed her undergraduate work at Duke University, graduate school at Georgia State University, internship at UTexas Health Science Center, and postdoctoral fellowship at Brown University. Her interests lie in the area of program development, treatment of severe psychiatric disorders in children, and psychotic spectrum disorders.

Photo Credits